ADDRESSING *THE SOCIETAL PROBLEM,*

"CORRUPTION"

&

CREATING VALUES IN

AFRICA

DISCIPLE ERAGA E. JACOB

DISCLAIMER:

The author and publisher of this book specifically renounce and disclaim any liability that is directly or indirectly incurred from the use of the contents of this book.

This publication is solely designed to provide much competed information concerning the subject matter covered by this book. The author and publisher are not also engaged in giving legal advice, if legal advice is required, the services of a professional should be sought.

<u>AIJ</u> is a registered trademark of Disciple Eraga E.Jacob organizations. If you purchase this book without the page covers, the book may have been stolen.

AKNOWLEDGEMENT

Where many have failed is where many have succeeded in life too. In every minute of success there are also numbers of years of struggle when someone may have failed. Failing is a default. It is just that success does not look back. I have fallen many times, before my risen.

Many have contributed to the risen and success of this book. Apparently my first tribute goes to my late Father. My mother, I say thank you. You stood in for me.

I am indebted to all my family members, friends, in-laws, Rich Dad &poor Dad, and people of the Faith that made this book a reality, include Mrs. Eraga Faith Lawrenta and my lovely children: Abraham, Isaac and Jacob Jnr.

Mrs. Faith Eraga is my helpmeet; she is a supporter of this project. I say thank you.

I thank the Spirit Filled Bible group, Jack W. Hayford, Why we want you to be Rich, Reinhard Bonnke for my exploit in contact with their both spiritual materials and intellectual property.

I give my most respectful thanks to Christians brothers and sisters include Pastor. Victor Maduadu and elders of the church that supported and accomplished the editorial work of this book

Special personal acknowledgment is also appropriated to *Amazon publishing, thank you for your insight. Your knowledge of publishing and printing is credible, and your vision for this endeavor has helped us in no small way in forging new dawn in the printing, publishing, and distribution of this book*

Lastly, to Jacob partners, I say thank you for your insight and hindsight, and for the launching coordination of this manual.

And my Readers, it has been so great. We could not have come this far without you all. Keep the balls rolling, keep learning, and continue the movement for the attainment of our expected positive change by addressing the societal evil called corruption and creating new values.

DEDICATION:

This Book is dedicated to Africa & to the whole World.

Copy Right

INTRODUCTION:

This book is divided into three Sections for the readers's ease. **PART ONE** is the subject matter: CORRUPTION IN THE ECONOMY & POLITICS OF AFRICAL

PART TWO *is about* the Societal Problems of Corruption, & Creating Values, while

PART THREE is on "the values we create & share." which help to mitigates corruption and indecency of all forms.

Corruption is at everywhere on earth, but it is deeply rooted in most parts than the other. This corruption something has not only surfaced in looting of material things and money but also in utterances or in words.

Africa/ Nigeria and some other nations need hygiene both in the word and in the political terrain, meaning that we should all repent from corruption of looting and in words so that we should able to speedily witness positive growth and fast development and peace in the World.

The subject of corruption deserves our attention all times. Corruption is at everywhere and it has adversely affected Africa and many other parts of the world resulting to suffering and crises. This must be addressed.

Africa is the most unfortunate because it is poor in and out, and it can only recover and retain its dignity when it does away with corruption. Repentance results into righteousness and righteousness exalts a family or a nation. In an exalted nation are people exalted by God as the book of 1 Corinthians. 15:34 aptly captured: "Awake to righteousness, and do not be corrupt for some do not know God. I speak this to your shame".

No religion encourages corruption and indecency. Corruption fight is a holy war, but the problem we are facing is that many governments and leaders who are supposed to lead by good examples are fighting corruption without actually fighting it.

This book is spiritually powered for <u>deliverance</u> from that menace by addressing the single societal problem (corruption) that has engendered all forms of afflictions to humanity mostly in Africa where both political and social hygiene is necessary to reduce the level of poverty, crimes rate, sicknesses, and deseases.

This book will open every prison door, and stop every lake of fire. It is a light in the darkness and it overshadows it. You will undoubtedly get it clear and right here. If we all sweep our homes, the whole world will be properly clean.

We pray together that God will open _our hearts_ for the entrance of His word against corruption practice in this book. May the fear of God take possession of our hearts and give us the grace to read all through this book to be able to catch the anchored message of this book with positive mind without picking offenses.

CONTENTS

Chapter Twenty-One

Abortion is wrong

Chapter Twenty-Two

Which House will you build

 in Exchange for thou Soul?

Chapter Twenty-Three

Disciplinary Action is a Weapon for Living Right

Chapter Twenty-Four

The Perplex

PART ONE:

CORRUPTION IN THE ECONOMY,

&

POLITICS,

CHAPTER ONE

ADDRESSING THE SOCIETAL PROBLEM, CORRUPTION

Scriptures clearly warned us that we shall see corruption, corrupt religions, leaders, followers, false converts and many more

It shall only grow worse from here if great men fail to come out boldly and speak the right word. *We must expose this evil (corruption) and spread the message of goodness, grace, truth, and righteousness.*

Deceitful people of this world are everywhere with different teachings spreading lies and also taking prominent government positions in many nations. Those kinds of people are seen in the Bible as people who had sunk deep into corruption, as in the days of Gibeah (Hosea. 9:9). God will remember their wickedness and punish them for their sins.

Woe to the sinful nation, a people whose guilt is great, a brood of evildoers, children given to corruption! They have forsaken the LORD, spurned the Holy One of Israel and turned their backs on Him (Isaiah1: 4)

Life eternal is not in corruption and is excellent in the mystery of godliness (1. Timothy 3). There is nothing good about corruption. Is it not because of our evil deed the nations are suffering from endless crises!

1 Timothy 3.1-5 addressed and warned us, saying: You must realize, however, that in the last days difficult times will come, people will be lovers of themselves, lovers of money, boastful, arrogant, abusive, disobedient to their parents, ungrateful, unholy, unfeeling, uncooperative, slanderous, degenerating, brutal, hateful of what is right, traitors, reckless, conceited, and lovers of pleasure rather than lovers of God. This is what most people turn

out to when they are entrusted with political power today.

I wrote this book to break my vow not to remain silent on public affairs. As at One night when the Lord spoke to Paul in a vision: "Do not be afraid; keep on speaking, do not be silent" (Acts 18: 9). My emergence into public life allay our concern- corruption in places of worship, leadership, and finances

If the religion and political price of our ascension to the highest office is to be silent in the midst of evils; the price is low and unreasonable.   This is the reason I have presented to us this testament to save us from the destroyer (corruption) of this world.

I believe with what you have heard so far you should be able to go ahead in reading this book to forge new dawn so that we address this huge problem together.

Corruption is the mother of poverty. Poverty is a burden to those who know the value of wealth. I hate poverty because it deprives one's access to livelihood and freedom. Let this embarrassment motivates us into fighting the battle of corruption in Africa, doing artworks to meet our needs and to live the Africa and Nigeria of our dream.

CHAPTER TWO

A LEADER WITH GOOD TRACK RECORDS

A steward is for his master, but in the case of leadership, the master becomes the steward. Always strive to be a good steward. An ambassador is a niche of his master or to whom he represents.

A leader is a special kind of person that leads while others follow. A leader supposes to be a light in the darkness by which others see. When the light is blinking, its followers get blind and when a leader is in darkness followers are in vast darkness and beeps.

A good leader cares for the well being of his people. This is the secret to making a working team call the followers to do their very best for heart blowing progress we desire. But today, some leaders and the followers make no difference. If a leader is bad, it is assume that his followers are rotten.

Leaders are our examples, and they should always lead by good examples.

A true person character is known when he takes a dominion. This attitude is the desired character that every leader should sacrifice worldliness on attainment for his followers.

We all know of many leaders in the world that had enough money, they attained high financial success status without honor. We all know there may be prime leaders that are lonely. We all know people who had 100 convoy cars, but today they lack honor. They have lost out like mush-room overnight. Mush -Rooms grow quickly overnight and decays overnight.

Life is not about gathering money into one's pocket, grasping here and grasping there for ourselves and children and building fences. Life is not only about what we have, but it also about what we do to others.

Someone can educate the whole world without having a classroom (a fence) if his/her intention is to create impactful values and make a positive impact. Success is not about gathering wealth without end. Success is helping others to be progressive and successful, loved, happy and peaceful.

Some past leaders did it. Their today dream is to correct the wrong they did but they cannot again because no one ever eats his cake and still have it. *One might have stolen the public funds because of love of it, but it is insecurity and poverty. I see this serious work.*

Remember! When someone is the only one that is rich among the poor thousands, no matter his generosity he may still be at danger so make others rich to be free from poverty and insecurity.

Now, I want you to free your mind. You might say this author addressing the Societal Problem (the evil call corruption) don't respect. We *are the subject matter in this exercise.* The change we want begins with us.

Regardless of whether we are rich or poor, smart or not smart, Ibo or Hausa, Yoruba or Niger Delta, Tiv or Ibo, Fulani or Hausa , negroes or Hebrews and Arabs by nation, the one common denomination will all have is the same identity of being visitors in this world. No one claim monopoly of the earth. We all want Nigeria, Africa and the World to be great and remain united.

The problem we have today is much worse than it has been because of the inept attitude and corrupt practice of leaders and followers.

I keep asking:

Which tower will you build to the sky? Which estates, private jets, or whatsoever name is it called that has never been heard? Remember that we are going back to the soil with nothing because we came here with nothing.

We need good leaders.Not necessary saints from birth but also those that have run around and finally learned a good lesson. A leader is a role model that guide and lead others to progress.

Let us try to start thinking as nations, as individual than to slowly sink into an ocean. Let us not succumb to big group-think approach, which is just a bad way of sinking our nations into the deep ocean.

What Africa needs are good leaders. What Nigeria need is leaders and followers with a dream. What is our dream!

The dream is to be free from corruption. If Nigeria will be free from poverty, it must first free from corruption, and then the world will rise.

The reason the world has not risen and settled is because Africa has refused to rise.

CHAPTER THREE

POLITICS IN AFR ICA HAS NOT MET GOOD LEADERSHIP STYLE

Many countries in Africa are practicing traditional democracy/politics.

Leadership Act in Africa does not conform to Godly leadership requirements and practices.

Political Leadership is not a personal affair rather; a power entrusted to someone motivated by service to curtail corruption/ evils to be able to provide for the people's need for orderliness in the society. The essence of political leadership is to serve humanity. This is one of the reasons it is said "The greatest among you must be a servant" (Matthew. 23:11)

The reason why every community/ state needs a leader is to control and prevent anarchy, lawlessness, and violence. In the absence of good and quality leadership, what we experience is anarchy.

Political hygiene is, therefore, necessary for Africa.

Leadership must be motivated by the basic concept 'service'. The greatest among us must be a servant. As it is written , instead, let the greatest among you become as the youngest, and the leader as one who serves (Luke. 22:25-27 is paraphrased)

Christianity refuses leadership responsibility to anyone who is not a nice person because when that kind of person becomes a leader, he may not abound with pleasing scenery to curb corruption and meet the needs of those who have no legitimate family support and the societal needs: protections of life and property, and taught morality.

A leader must learn how to reprove covetousness, encourage discipline and meets the societal needs. If we cannot lead ourselves, we cannot lead others. If we cannot discipline ourselves we will not be able to discipline other people; if you are not peaceful, you will not have peace to give to others. It is about you first.

It takes pure heart and love to be a good leader. A good leader is focus, determined, proactive, and foresighted and committed to his people. A leader should be a kind person that can control himself and others. It takes a leader a long time to react. It is ordinary men that react before they think.

Politics in many parts of the world matches no Christianity leadership style. Christian's leadership style is never tolerated or practiced in the most parts of the world. Even when a Christ-like person assumes the mantle of leadership, those who are outsides his faith and thinking box corrupt it and makes it difficult and miserable.

All God's people are therefor encouraged to constantly pray for those who have authority and responsibility for us throughout Africa and the world for good leadership.

CHAPTER FOUR

HOW TO GET FAMOUS/ POPULARITY INTO POLITICAL OFFICES:

1. **Fear of God:** Fear the Lord your God and it shall be well with you. It was God alone that led Joseph to the second command rank in Egypt. In the absence of God, we can do nothing. With God, all things are possible (Eccl.12: 12). With the fear of God, we get all things we might ask him for. In the absence of men; remember that there is nothing too hard for God. It was God alone that also led Jacob in the desert.

2. **Address Public Issues:** A wise man said, with that, I walked on stage to introduce my friend to thousands of families and students. Look for a person to take you to the stage of students, families, with the opportunity to address national issue politely without mincing

words in what you believe you can do and stand with accuracy.

3. **Learning: B**e an apprentice to a renowned and sincere person with your political interest. Look for supportive people who will push you to success? That is an opportunity for you.

4. **Have good negotiations skill and patient:** Politica negotiation is not short and quick as in commercial negotiation. Have good negotiation skills with the patient to wait.

4. **Have a battle Field:** Every dream has its battle field. Fight your fight at the right battlefield for victory. Every victory is a plus for another victory that is yet to come. There is no dream too big to achieve. Have a battle field for your dream. That is it.

5. **Be personal:** Don't only depends on group thinking. Group thinking is good because it

sometimes pulls a crowd to you, but it should not always be something you do.

Break up the herd before you become incapable of seeing, hearing and thinking proper. Do it yourself. People who are capable of thinking for themselves will rarely be part of any herd or group thinking on a very sensitive decision.

Serious people stand alone in some issues to win in argument; when they know, they are right. This builds confidence.

Only you should break camel's head.

6. **The Media:** The mass media is a powerful tool for good and for bad, so the bottom line is: you have to learn to think for yourself properly to forge ahead before the media think for you.

The media is very fast and universal. They float you or decide to sink you. Befriend them and be very careful with the Medias.

Is it okay?

Make sure all social media channels are engagement friendly. This include your website, face book, go-goo, and glass door channels. Don't promise what you are not sure you can do, and don't say what you are not sure.

7. **Have fans.** Fans are decorators and whirlwind that blows dust up and down for you. They go before you to clear radicals and thorns out of your roads.

8. **Be Knowledge Based:** Have knowledge and truth based polity, with this you remain strong and unopposed. Nothing overshadows light (knowledge).

8. **Pray and Watch:** In all things put God first. Always pray & watch (don't close your eyes when you pray. How do you see?), think and act appropriately. There is absolutely nothing the Lord cannot do. With the above tips, you can become a good leader and sustain it.

9. **Have clear goals, objective and commitment:** There must be an emotional commitment between the potential leader and the potential followers which followers engaged with the leader for the country.

Potential followers need to hear why they should want to elect and work with you, why you are the best, how they will feel when they elect you and work with you.

A country is only actively in support and ready to work with a potential leader that excites and interests them.

Engagement in government service demands open communication of facts, clear goals and well understood objectives. Don't have the mistake of promising a person or groups what you are not sure you can do.

A leader must understand what the citizens think by using tools which include social media and online forums, encouraging open discussion and debate and giving people a voice. This is what great nations and personality do.

CHAPTER FIVE

CORRUPTION IN THE WORLD

As a Jew and a Bible person, I see corruption fighting as a Holy War. For it is written: *You will not let your Holy One see corruption/evil (Psalm 16: 10)*

Corruption is the saying and the doing of a wrong thing for personal benefit. What is not right is wrong and no wrong can make right.

Corruption is in every evil thought, word, and action that breeds evil result even when this evil motive is to get the right thing done. What is wrong cannot be right. Corruption is when someone is holding fast to what is wrong, and doing it for a selfish motive, e.g. bribery, looting, fake promise, aiding and abetting, lying pen, etc. To give a bribe is corruption and to receive it is another corruption. Any unrighteousness is corruption/evil.

KINDS OF CORRUPTION:

(A). *financial corruption:* This involves looting and stealing of money- directly or indirectly.

(B). *Corruption in words-* This is when a person is corrupt in words (Corruption of the word).Fake political promises is an instance of this kind of corruption. People with <u>good intentions make</u> promises, but *it takes those with integrity and the fear of God* to make them a reality and keep them. Don't promised people what you are not sure you can do.

(C). *Aiding and Abetting corruption is corruption.* Stop hiding in pajamas.How can your worker be stealing without knowing. Why are you a supervisor or a leader? We don't aid and abet corruption.

CHAPTER SIX:

CORRUPTION OF THE WORD

Some people are not only corrupt in the way they go about finances but also in the word (corruption of the word).

Is it not because their heart and words are corrupt that they twist the law, policy, codes of conducts and given it a different meaning to suite their unhealthy desire? This stirs arguments, jealousy, and slander and brings division.

When a sincere person comes in to make things right, he will be called different names. To the spoiler, that kind of good behavior is a mere godliness and devil interface, and he is seen as a person who wants to be rich/ wealthy and the spoiler's prayer point turns to evil prayer, wishing the person untimely death. Those kinds of people have an unhealthy desire to quibble over truth and cause troubles. Their minds are corrupt, and their words are rotten.

To them doing good work are offenses because it may stop their corruption, unethical behavior and unprofessional way of doing things.

The Bible tells us to keep the mouth free from perversity and to keep corrupt talk far from the lips (Proverbs. 4.24). Do not be deceived evil communications corrupt good manners (1 Corinthians 15.33). This is a corruption in the word.

Psalm 14:1 says, the *fool has said in his mind, there is no God. They are corrupt and commit evil deeds; not one of them practices what is good. Woe to those who call evil good and good evil, who put darkness for light and light for darkness, who put bitter for sweet and sweet for bitter! (Isaiah.5: 20).*The original meaning of the word, policy, constitution is twisted to suite their selfish interest. This is another form of corruption.

For instance, where is the proper federation of Nigeria as obtained in the 1960 and 1963 constitution? The constitution says Nigeria should be run along Federal lines to be able to curb impurities and to experience real peace. This has being twisted.

Is it not because the heart is corrupt that they twist meaning? Discrimination, tribalism, and racism do not come naturally; it is taught, planted and watered. This is a corruption of the word.

Religions heads and government leaders should desist from changing meanings. Political Leaders should stop telling lies, and promising us fake promises; this is another corruption (a corruption of word).

C. *Aiding/abetting corruption:*

Aiding and abetting of corruption is another corruption– This is when a leader or a follower is not supervising or being supervised, then watching each other activity in pretense as a leader or a follower. This is indiscipline; when we are twisting translations and interpretations of the word, policy, constitution etc. It also includes when someone turns back and closes eyes on people who are stealing that deserve investigation for onward actions.

CHAPTER SEVEN

OBSTRUCTIONS /BARRIERS TO FIGHTING CORRUPTION

(1).The fighter must be healthy, knowledgeable, bold and financially balanced/ rich. If the fighter does not have money to fight, corrupt people may find victory.

(2). It is a long time fight and investment. The impact is not quick and seen in a short time; as a result, people do not cherish it.

(3). impatient: Many are not patient about fighting corruption; to them, it is a further waste of time, resources and energy.

(4). It is capital intensive since it requires restructuring and also blocking people who are corrupt into public offices entrance.

(5). It can lead to further corruption and violence if not jointly supported and handled carefully.

(6).A Perceived scam and dishonesty on the side of a leader by his/ her followers will aggravate further corruption practice that cannot be control.

CAUSES OF CORRUPTIONS:

- Indiscipline, Lack of integrity and principal values

- Lack of good leadership by good examples.

- Poor control and supervision of deligated duties and responsibilities

- Lack of vision, and high expectations due to over fake promises

- Lack of effective policies and regulations.

- A corrupt word corrupts people. Note! Faith comes by hearing. What is heard from the lips can build or destroyed

- Poverty

  - Big gap between the poor and the rich, sumptuous living...etc

CHAPTER EIGHT

HOW TO FIGHT CORRUPTION BY A LEADER

- By teaching and preaching against it with good action example.

- Be a person of integrity and discipline. You can only do little things with some integrity and some discipline, but with complete discipline, you can do all things. Integrity is 100%; 95.99% integrity is no integrity.

- Start the change with yourself. The change we want begins with us.

- Make every of your action plan a purpose driving one, swiss and transparent

- Make clear your economic policies and let every body know your driven/intention. You can write it in white and share it. This makes your vision clearer.

- Be a true democrat so that you can carry oppositions along; but also learn how to stand alone on certain issues.

- Seek for supporters who are ready to drive with you the same purpose/ vision

- Listen to oppositions, their criticisms, and suggestions then take them to the screen and filter them because in inside every gossip there is something good to learn there from. It is not every word of an opposition that is meant to hurt.

- The essence of opposition is to validate our actions/lapses for our improvement. They contribute to our rising. Note, as they keep saying negative things about us, people step forward to see what we are doing.

- Appoint your oppositions and fix them in the areas they are complaining about to work with you. They Will not accept the work if they have evil intentions meaning that they are corrupt. Let them go so that you will not lose your F-O-C-U-S. Always stand to what you believe. This is your confidence.

- Let their criticism and your action plan be your mirror to be able to measure your performance.

- Redeem your time (See: Jeremiah 8:8, Deuteronomy 31:25-29, 2 Peter 2: 15). There is no time at all to waste because people would like to see result per quarter.

- Test every thing and hold fast to what is good (1 Thessalonians 5: 21)

- Deliberate Repentance- repentance is not an option. It becomes a must for a leader to be able to rule with the fear of God and fight corruption. No one can out run God no matter how knowledgeable he may be

- Very stringent economic policies and laws should be made open to people in an expressly written form to avoid ignorance and seek support.

We have created an environment that accommodates ill -gotten wealth. This must be stoped. With this, we are fighting corruption without actually fighting it. Corruption is fought successfully through collaboration. It should be every body's agenda. There must be a sense of togetherness.

-   Corruption should be seen as an illegal business by our government and take procurement policies serious. We should stop celebrating the wrong people and close the avenues and channels for cantering away with our money. Those that hold public offices should not have foreign domiciliary accounts without justification.

CHAPTER NINE

HOW TO DETER OTHERS FROM FURTHER CORRUPTION:

All unrighteousness is a big wound to a nation. It can lead to separation/ division since it ends in endless suffering, difficulties, and violence. How do we respond to/address such deep and gaping situation? The answer is in humility expected of a man as expressly obtainable in the word of God. The pattern for this recovery must involve spiritual dimension:

- **Confession-** every looter/ corrupt man have to acknowledge the unjust and hurtful actions toward other people and the nation

- **Repentance:** Accept that you were guilty after confession, and turn from unloving actions to loving actions.

- **Restitution:** Meaning to restore that which has been damaged, destroyed and seeking justice with the authorities.

- **Reconciliation:** this is to express forgiveness which the repented sinner in turn received and now pursue intimate fellowship with God and men. This is how to heal the wound inffections.

Do not just go with the money, consulting profiled lawyers and asking for forgiveness without restitution. Restitution brings true forgiveness and reconciliation.

CHAPTER TEN

OUR EDUCATION SYSTEM

Don't be deceived. The standard of education in public schools has dropped severely. It is beginning to lose total value.

Standards are measure in the education system. Public schools are performing below average. In summary, our country's education system is getting worse. Many of the schools from playgroup to tertiary institutions are rated poor in the world. This is not caused by lack of money because, in the federal government, vast amount of money is annually budgeted to run and maintain those schools. But they do not have a robust will power to impair a change and right. This is the problem we have.

There are 36 states in Nigeria and the federal capital territory- Abuja. All the public schools scattered among the states have an average grade in their rating in the following areas:

(a)Standard and accountability

(b) School's climates

(c) Teacher quality development

(d) Adequacy in learning facilities and school infrastructures etc

The Nigeria schools run by our government resist a change due to corruption. As I have said earlier ,this is not as a result of lack of funds. It is as a result of corruption. The money budgeted for education system is not well spent and used for its purpose.

People who had no choice are still attending those schools while those who are in charge of running the schools go abroad to study and also send their children there to study. This is demoralizing and indication that focus and value is lost in our education system

DISCIPLE ERAGA JACOB'S VIEW & ANSWER:

Nigeria government does not give detail attention to public schools to know how the schools are being run for accountability. Federal government agents in charge and control of federal schools should effect controls and fight corruption in the public schools by monitoring them. Comrade Adam Oshomole of Edo State, Nigeria did this when he was a governor.

He is an excellent example of a leader/people taking action and accomplishing something. He takes the matter into his hands instead of waiting for someone else to do something about it. It is unconventional, but it seems to be working. Determined artists are the only people around who have that zeal and live by example no matter where they live and what they do.

You might think this book is disrespectful. It is not so. I wrote this book to help us realize what we have done wrong, where we have failed and to know what to do next for us to be out of the mess we put ourselves.

Nigerians need life touching word in this our defining moment or era, a life quickening word that will establish the African continent's dominion once.

To learn more teaching on how to eradicate corruption, and in Africa system, please gogoo: "Political hygiene is necessary for Africa by the professor. " Molumba of Kenya". Much more is also discussed of this topic (corruption) in the last pages of this book. Stay tuned.

CHAPTER ELEVEN

UNVEILING THE MASK COVERING THE MASQUERADE:

PENSIONS FUNDS CONTRIBUTIONS SCHEME IN AFRICA

This pension scheme introduced among employees which has replaced the retirement benefit plan in many organizations is a monster problem, a huge one.

Pension savings scheme introduced into Nigeria working force to replace the retirement benefits plan is like a paper home on the top of a gallery that is tore down when the wind blows.

Employers and institutions managing the funds on behalf of employees are making more money and get more luxurious with the pensions funds to the detriment of the savers or employees that make the contributions and an owner of it.

The saver's funds are not compounded, reinvested, and remitted as at when due, e.g. when worker's salaries deducted for the month of October- December 2017 is paid to the pension's funds account in June 2018, and at last, this contribution cannot take care of pensioners long because the fund does not accrue interest. Time value of money is not known here and the pensioner suffers when the money is finished. There is corruption here.

It is not a lifetime retirement benefits plan. Nigeria government should quickly review this practice and correct the remittances corruption something between the employers and the pension funds management against workers. I want us to be safe.

Our Economic challenge (corruption & poverty) is brought by the way we think about money; we have to be wise in the way we use and plan with money and think in money matter.

When I remember where I am coming from, and at where I am today and the next place I will certainly be, you would like to read this book for an end.

I think the two big subjects I was weak at school are what I do better today. That was English and commerce, but today I am a minister, I write books in English, and I also trade as a merchant seeking goodly pearl. Where you think you are not important might be where your life will blossom in impacting lives. Divine idea is the major thing we need to blossom progressively in our endeavors.

Remain open to ideas; a small spark in the brain ignites a fire. The entire big things we see around us were very tiny ideas developed.

Below is titanic,

Whenever you may talk about starting your own small company your manager slow you down, that it is against the policy to own a business while already working.

I want you to have a better chance of retiring without a financial struggle. Majority of Nigeria workers are on contract jobs. Contract staff will face significant financial challenges when they are out of their services in the future. This new pension scheme will not help them.

It is because of the future challenge of likely not able to save enough through the pension scheme program and not using it wisely to yield interest I am unveiling this mask covering the considerable masquerade dancing ahead of you.

How those short services employees and contract staff welfare is going to be in the future is very uncertain. They will face a horrible financial war. I recommend to them here to be creative and innovative. I also recommended that they engage in artwork with their spare time, augmenting their earnings.

Let us also quickly see the Nigeria job creation N-power Social initiative Programme of 2016. This Jobs creation and employment initiative social investment program of the Nigeria Government is a very good one, but it may be deceptive and non impactful if it is not well handled.

Anything that is not manage well cannot be reliable, and it does not transform lives mostly when it lacks a process and determined goal. N-Power may end up not achieving its goal of a social initiated program designed to encourage the youth into creativity for economic development, meaning to create jobs, bring entrepreneurial spirit among the youth and for poverty alleviation but also as a tool for economic growth through youth empowerment.

It is a good mission originally drafted to create jobs and to encourage the youth into creativity, entrepreneurship, and productivity but it would not last if it is not for youth skills development and creativity for productivity. It may turn out to a political strategy to the ascension of prominent political offices. It becomes a paper house on a rock/ or mountain top. Anything can happen to that kind of house

Jobs are created by creating new jobs not by filling vacant positions and making youth apprentices to the states government employees in the various state government ministries. Many of those N- Power workers have no jobs to do because the jobs were not indeed created based on expansion or on the creation of the new jobs on the platform of creating new ministries and industries. N- Power is a good vision, but a good vision can become a bad one when it is wrongly driven and lack a genuine process. A nation without a good drive and process can be finding progress without actually seeking it.

Today training in our schools is changing. Many technical schools, polytechnics, and Universities now have business schools for those interested in building their businesses. We do not have practical lessons to learn in the business study at schools, but we learn much in practice. Class Paperwork is not the same thing as in practice. Until when we put it into practice outside the classroom else, the education/ training will not mean much.

I believe this is what N-Power is also out to fix.

The youth are disturbed and having sleepless nights waiting for the government jobs they have not seen. I think this is the problem the N-Power is meant to address- creativity, jobs creations, self-development / entrepreneurship.

However, what we see is deception. How doe Federal government creates jobs that cannot exceed their tenure in the office? No jobs have been created but a coded way of sharing the national cake among the few lucky people. This is what I saw.

I am writing to address this concern here. It is not only about the youth N- Power; also a concern is the country general layoff problem.

Do not wait for our leaders or government. Our government is telling us lies about nonexisting jobs and their jobs creation for the youth.

The government is worse off than what the government is telling us today. With the resources we have, our country is still very bright if honest people who are concerned to make great of our country are entrusted with leadership positions.

If the youth do not stop expecting the government to do everything for them too, we will continue to have the same results. We become a nation filled with well-educated people looking for jobs and free meals, and financially needy. Giving youth the check to eat today and suffer tomorrow will not solve the problem. Instead teach them how to do something through creativity and innovation. This will help us out of this mess we put ourselves.

N- Power program may temporally push forward the problem of unemployment if not well handled. The truth is that the jobs are not actually being created and the existing jobs assumed to have been created are too vulnerable.

How will somebody without teaching training at school be employed to teach at school? If we hired untrained teachers for our children, the children may come out with f9 and may later turn out to ruffians, and rubbing hands.

 Albert Einstein defined insanity as "doing the same thing over and over again and expecting different results." In this case, it is my opinion that it is insanity to pay youth salaries without jobs / sending them to workshop for business and skills acquisition. Our schools do not teach them how to create wealth and use money (commercial usage Literacy), so we have horrible commercial usage life style.

There are many gifted youth who will never be discovered because they have never been developed. Deceiving our youth with free salaries for not doing any work or being trained on how to create wealth is vast darkness.

There are over one billion minerals that are untapped in them. Develop their skills and make them see life beyond sitting idle in the offices and in the cubicles.

We want them to be creative, rather than expect a handout from the government. That is how we can help to solve the problem of unemployment.

Apparently this book cannot help everyone, but it can help those who genuinely have the desire to experience a turnaround through creativity. Creative thinking is conceptual and constructive reasoning that helps to bring and keep an idea on a track or position. This is also called productive thinking. This process is also missing

We must be careful about the kind of teaching, and education we give or receive. Many people want the government or people to always do everything for them. I think the major things the government owns us is free education, job, security of life and property, provision of water and light, and healthcare. The government does not own you your Vision and willingness. These are two critical things you must have and control by yourself to succeed progressively.

The youth should have vision, and our leaders should dream pleasant dreams. Mrs. Kim goal is for all women to increase their financial IQ and not depend on men to take care of them. I would recommend her book (a Rich woman by Kim, Robert's wife) for both men and women in Nigeria, Africa, and others because reading the book can help to develop the spirit of artistry.

If we as a nation attempt to solve the unemployment problem, social security and healthcare, and poverty by giving people more money free, free houses, payouts, the golden goose will be cooked and eaten once, that there will be no more golden eggs.

It is a deception in the apex. Let us do the right things to save our country by genuinely creating the kind of environment and works by encouraging innovation and creativity for self-reliance among the youth.

'My message is clear,

' with zero tolerance

in financial and none

financial corruption

we can build our nations

high and ride on horses,

become richer and peaceful

than getting poorer and

borrowing day by day Instead

of giving good help to others'.

CHAPTER TWELVE

ADDRESSING RELIGIONS' MATTER IN THE WORLD, AFRICA, AND NIGERIA

MY RELIGIOUS PHILOSOPHY: Since we are addressing our societal problems here for peace, love, and happiness, we shall be addressing the problem of just two major religions in the World today, i.e., Christianity and Islam in this book.

I firmly believe in the freedom of religion. All religion prays. Everybody has a choice too when it comes to a religion matter. This means there should be no force in religion. The Quran says, there shall be no compulsion in religion (Tura. 2:256).

In my opinion, the idea of killing and seeing others as evil because of religion is naïve, wickedness that needs severe spiritual war. Whether you are a Jew, Christian or Muslim hold to your faith and stop looking for someone to kill in the name of a religion.

I believe in the supremacy of God. I believe in his son-ship and also in the Holy Spirit. And they are one.

That: God created the heavens and the earth in the beginning (Genesis.1:1-2) and all which the heavens and the earth are contained.

That: ...Grace and truth were brought by Jesus (John 1: 17), to empower us so that we can resist every unrighteousness and every resistant of that truth and grace.

That: who so ever shall embrace the same shall have earthly blessing here as it is, in heaven where eternity is.

I believe in God the Father, in the son (JESUS), and in the Holy Spirit and in their unity.

WHAT SUSTAINS FAITH AND TRUTH ON EARTH

(a) Grace and the truth.

(b) The word and sacrifice

(c) The Holy Spirit

(d) The blood of Jesus

(e) Prayer and fasting

CHRISTIANS' INSTRUMENTS FOR SPIRITUAL WAR:

- The name: Jesus

- The mystery of the flesh and the Blood of Jesus- holy communion

- Acting the mystery with the word of God

- Prayer and fasting

- Offering and sacrifice as Moses was commanded

- Mantle

- The annointed water and oil

CHAPTER THIRTEEN

MY VIEW ABOUT CHRISTIANITY, ISLAM AND OTHER RELIGIONS

I respect people that do not practice my religion and hold unto their belief because we all have the right and freedom to belong to a religion of our choices; but we are not allowed to cause war and destruction with it. It is only true religion seeks righteousness, peace, freedom, unity, and life eternal.

Islam: I believe that the religions exist, that it means *peace* as I was told and I see only peace in the Quran when I am reading it; but my faith is in Christianity. I have a copy of the Quran with me at home. I sometimes create time to read it so that nobody deceives me. We do not fight anybody over a religion matter. We leave religion and faith battle to God.

The Quran, in *Tura 2:256 says: There shall be no compulsion in religion.* True guidance is now distinct from error. He that renounce the idols and know his faith in Allah shall grasp the firmest handle that will never break. Allah is hearing, all knowing.

That: Allah guided by his will those who believe in the truth which had been disputed (Tura 2:213).

Allah guides whom he will to the right path. Friends! Why are we fighting and killing each other? Submit all your bows and arrows.

You are not fighting for God. You are killing because of your greed and hatred which you have against your selves and even with God.

In chapter 1:1 the Quran says: in the name of Allah, the compassionate, the merciful...praise be to Allah ..., You alone we worship. Here Muslims says "praise be to God" And He alone they worship, meaning that they praise and worship only God without <u>idols</u> and Christians does it too according to their faith and doctrine.

What is the problem? Why are you killing worshipers during praises and worship in the churches and Mosques? Stop the killing. Human beings may look and worship differently.

Some may be bad, and many may be good, some are weak, and some have greater firepower than others, but none is permitted to take another's life. We are born to love and peaceful. Discrimination and racism do not come naturally; it is taught, planted and watered. This is corruption in words.

Some religious leaders should desist from teaching and preaching evil and hatred through twisting meaning. It is a corruption of the mind and in the word.

What is wrong in praise and Worship as ordained by God? Quran 69:52 says "… It is the despair of the unbeliever. It is the incubi truth. Praise, then, the name of your Lord, the Almighty"

What is wrong in praise? All creatures are continuously praising God even when we do not understand their languages or ways. Benignant is He and forgiving (Quaran17:44). Stop killing in the name of religion. It is an unforgivable sin to take another's life. Who are you a mere man to criticize contradiction and fight back for God?

What is written is eternal. I have preached the message to you as I was given for the truth to be established. This testament bears us witness. This is the reason I have written so that we repent. Stop killing about.

QUESTIONS:

What do you know in Christianity?

What do you know in Islam as a religion?

YOUR RESPONSES: info.jeafservices@gmail.com

....

....

....

....

....

....

CHAPTER FOURTEEN

WHAT MY PARENTS TOLD ME

(1)

MY FATHER:

He introduced the world to me. He told me the world is not straight. He said this world has a beginning and it may have an end, meaning: One was born and one is to die. To be born is to have a journey to go and to die is to end the journey started.

He told me that the world is whole, good and beautiful but what is in it do corrupt it. He told me not to corrupt it, that evil did goes round and come around.

He beat me sometimes when I refused to take his instruction / when I disobeyed my Mummy as a child. It is not that he was harsh.

Why beating me Daddy? I once asked him. "I want you to experience how the world will treat you when you refused to do the right thing and repeated the same offense.

He advised me to learn how to do the right thing for me to have the right thing in this world on my table.

He also told me that there is seed time and there is harvest time, that what a man sows shall he reap "This is a law."He added.

One of the difficult times I ever had with him as a child was that my father was a disciplined teacher. No one misbehaved when Daddy was around. So he disciplined me whenever I proved to be stubborn.

When I noticed this, I go for self-discipline, I went for it. I am a disciplined person. Today my father is not here again, but he had shown me the right way I should go in life.

(2)

MY MOTHER:

My mother introduced me to the world. Unlike my father who introduced the world to me. She said: "this is my son treat him well. To have all the possibilities done my son, you must observe Nature and keep the divine laws.

I think this is the reason when she gave birth to me she took me to the church at childhood for consecration and dedication.

I was dedicated to God from the womb of my mother and after my birth in the Roman Catholics Church. The Priest gave me the name Jacob as the envoy of my parents in that time.

She told me that when I was in her womb, she used to pack white chalk and rub it in her womb praying that this child in her womb should be pure and holy. I am not surprised that I am a positive thinker. I am that kind of person with a clean mind.

My Mum advised me and said: guide your leg, your mouth, and your mind and above all fear thy LORD but be brave, and when you observe to do those things I tell you, all shall be well with you.

She recites the Rosary (Holy Mary mystical prayers) with the slogan, "…Holy Mary, full of grace, the Lord is with you…" Those who do know their God shall not lack anything". I just spoke about my mother and my father. What did your father and your mother told you?

A.

What did your father tell you?

....

....

B.

What did your Mother tell you?

CHAPTER FIFTEEN

OUR ACHIEVABLE DREAM

There is progress everywhere in the world, but Nigeria is not in line with this progress now. Good government or state is not built in a day. It requires constant attention and maintenance from both leaders and followers all day, every day. It has to be part of our culture

Where is Nigeria's voice in the World Trade Organization (W T O)?

Today is full of ever-changing technology and update is necessary. Where is Nigeria the giant of Africa?

This is not the Nigeria of our dream. The first big homework Nigeria must do is in the area of agriculture to put food on the table of her citizens. With determination, she can export food items that can take care of many parts of the world rather than importing food items.

Where is the food and waters of land the Lord has given to us?

Great people address a nation through writing and speech but where is the voice of our nobles? Many have corrupted their words while many are misunderstood. This is not the Nigeria of our dream. Our dream is love, happiness, peace, and unity for progress.

CHAPTER SIXTEEN

OUR HEALTH CARE DELIVERY SERVICE

There is nothing to write home about our health care delivery service.

Our people flown abroad daily for this invisible service when they have health challenges for medical attention. Our health centers are collapsing. This is very shameful. Leaders are taken to abroad on health ground. Think about this. What happened to our clinics and hospitals colossal money (Billions) are budgeted and approved for maintenance every year? Walk around all the government clinics what is seen is non funtional Xray machines, …and disappointment.

Corruption has caused us much harm in the public hospitals and clinics. If our government is serious, let them also strip off importation of this invisible service as they often suddenly stopped the importation of other visible goods. This would help us keep our public hospitals and clinics well by our government functionaries for the common man.

Our government should put more effort on projects supervision for their implementation. Leaders are sleeping that is the reason followers are not working.

Disciples Eraga Jacob'sViews:

Our Country is corrupt. Corruption should be dealt with for every other thing to work well.

The problem in our various ministries is corruption. What are the conditions of our various ministries, either in commerce, agriculture, education, health, transport and aviation, power and industry e.t.c?

It is because of corruption we cannot experience the beauty of Nigeria. We need fire branded democrats in Africa to lead us to the Africa of our dream.

Followers are worse because leaders are bad. When a Leader is lousy, followers will be much more or worse. This is not the desire of Nigeria our hope and pride.

PART TWO:

Addressing the Societal Problems of Corruption

&

Creating Values In Africa

CHAPTER SEVENTEEN

SPIRITUAL WEAPONS FOR OVERCOMING CORRUPTION:

(a)

SPIRITUALITY

Spirituality is living a life that is free from canalitty. Spirituality secures a destiny for eternity. Be spiritual. When someone is not spiritual, he becomes well garnished; but empty. Don't be wanting in the things of God. To be walking outside God's desire is no life. Your spirituality is your lifting.

The importance of spirituality is that it saves us from temptation and tempting objects around us.

Spirituality helps salvation, focus, sensitivity, and accomplishment. There is no seriousness in life that is spent outside God's will. When someone is spiritual, he should be able to have remorse when entangled with temptation.

Spirituality helps to engage the ministry power of angels. There is no person of virtue on earth from the time of living in the cave who had not have an encounter with an Angel on the platform of living a spiritual life. They all enjoyed angels companionship on earth.

Abraham, Isaac, Jacob, Moses, Daniel, and Jesus all believed in the ministry of the Angels and Holy Spirit. Spirituality brings ideas and makes us well thinkers for a ride. Spirituality makes somebody a kind of person the riches of God dwell in abundance, and respected.

We ask God for the grace to be spiritual because spirituality makes us people who resemble Him and become somebody that resemble Christ in all ramifications (2Corintians. 5:17-19).

Spirituality enhances integrity, and causes us to resist temptations bravely, so that our victory may be honorable. It is integrity that enables us to attract others to the way of God and live corruption free life. Be spiritual.

(b)

LEAVE FLESH/CARNAL LIFE

When someone is living a flesh / carnal life, it is evident in anything he does. Flesh is the human nature that opposes God's will. The flesh is human nature in the form of a cell which is an enemy of godliness.

A man or a person who is seduced by human nature is said to be living in a sexual/flesh life. If someone allows secular knowledge, body's desire to lure him or her, it is flesh. This kind of person will hardly escape corruption since the person is controlled by circumstances.

Flesh is self or life spent outside God's will. This is a life that is possessed by human nature. This human nature (flesh) always craves for more and enjoys dead works.

Flesh (self) dwells and struggle with the soul. It dictates and enforces its will on the soul. The works of the flesh are evident. It has its method of motivating and accomplishing a mission.

What flesh does is plain. What this old man does shows itself in every indecency. The flesh is jealous and impure with constant efforts to always take the best and the worst to others. Corruption is the way of the flesh.

This old man can corrupt the soul and brings misery and poisoning venoms that cause death if not control. Flesh kills because it is a clutch of sin that possesses men. It is a spirit of greediness and close off.

Flesh intimidate others in order to gain control. It manipulates and takes advantage of others and concentrates on it to oppress them. Flesh does not give to others without a purpose, meaning, it does not give to free others.

Flesh witchcraft and bewitched to create insecurity until the oppressed or captive seeks the help of the witchcraft and trap the oppressed the more. Flesh seeks to Lord over another without the person's consent. The flesh uses demonic power to dislodge others and make them succumb to domination. witchurting others is bad.

"Self" creates a kind of pandemonium to appear a champion. When you see people become enemies, gossips each other and not wanting to see each other's face in a family, church, house, at a place of work, in government house, it is flesh that is at work.

People of the same lineage sideline faces from each one, and scattered in all things. Fleshes always fight for separation.

Flesh is that who is born of flesh, not of blood. God abhors this old man in whatever form it may manifest in someone. See Romans 6:8.

Flesh is carnal mind. If someone is carnal minded, even though he is seen believing he has to be born again. There is nothing call carnal believer and unbeliever. An unbeliever is a carnal man his end is the same with the 'carnal believer'.

Noone can hide carnality. You cannot hide it. The more we hide and do carnality, the more it is revealed, shown in our thoughts, and words.

Expose yourself to the truth and life of Christ. The flesh does what the Holy Spirit hates. When this human nature called the flesh is in control of somebody, it is evident.

It is hard and impossible to control the flesh except when the mercy of God prevails. When a person is delivered from the life of self, he becomes a righteous person. Without this, whatever it is that we do according to the counsel of this Old Man leads to destruction and death.

A man becomes an enemy of God when controlled by the flesh. The flesh hides to fight, smoke, and drink and to condemn.

The flesh praises Jesus today and dances for the same old man the next day. Flesh knows how to hide very well without being caught, but the joy is that Christ has prevailed and taken over.

The question that needs answer is this: "Who leads you?" Who leads us matters. Say no to corruption. The work of the flesh is visible, and it is fought by knowing God in the power of His grace given to us. So, be spiritual to be able to resist corruption because it will certainly come.

'I pray thee, Lord, if there is an area I have been found wanting as a child of God, may God forgive me and continue to take the lead of my life and yours.

(c)

GO FOR SALVATION

No one can resist evil without salvation, and then striving against sin. Are you truly saved?

If we neglect so great salvation conferred in us by God we can not resist the evil of corruption.

Indifference to salvation has caused havoc and great suffering to the human race. The benefits of salvation outweigh corruption. How great is salvation! Salvation is confirmed by three facts: (a) Jesus brought salvation (John. 1:17), (b) it was confirmed by his apostles (c), and it was attested to by the ministry of the Holy Spirit through miracles, signs, and wonders and it is age long. Follow God diligently (Exodus.15:26; Deuteronomy. 28:1) through salvation.

Always see things in God's perspective. Salvation is ultimate because it helps to minimize corruption. It delivers to us the blessings of God.

How shall we escape if we neglect so great a salvation, which at first began to be spoken by the Lord Jesus, which was confirmed to us by those (apostles) who heard Him? God is also bearing witness both with signs and wonders with various miracles, and gifts of the Holy Spirit according to His own will (Hebrews. 2:3-4).

Salvation is real. If our treasures are not in the hands of the Lord, they are not safe. Say no to evil/ corruption.

Salvation is the greatest. Yesterday is not yours again but today is yours. Today and tomorrow are yours to determine to be good. May the Lord satisfy us and bless us forever and ever.

(d)

BE A KIND MAN AFTER GOD'S HEART:

The man after God's heart is the man in God's design with pure heart and incorruptible beauty, gentle and quiet in spirit.

He is a spiritual man endued with great understanding. He lives his life in justice and his hope in GOD is his hidden place in the days of trouble. He grows every day in the spiritual things and love. He trusts God and is victorious.

It is complicated and very dangerous to fight someone who is after God's heart. No one can toss him around because God leads him.

You are no longer a child tossed to and fro and carrying about by every wind and craftiness. Being a kind man of God is great and frees us from corruption.

Paul the Apostle clearly described what becomes of a man after God's heart: "That we should no longer be children tossed to and fro and carried about with every wind of doctrine, by the trickery of men, in the cunning craftiness of deceitful plotting, but speaking the truth in love… (Ephesians. 4:14). Meaning, when we know God, we flee corruption and live a freer life.

(e)*WALKING IN THE GRACE OF GRACE*

Grace is an unmerited favor, the unconditional acceptance and empowerment that we receive from God (Eph. 1:6; 1 Corinth. 15:10). Grace (*Chari)* is God's nature in a man that propels his obedience, and lifted him beyond what he cannot do and achieve by technical knowledge, strength, and self-understanding.

Grace is God's special privilege enjoyed by man to live right. It is the supernatural ability seen as the miraculous that keeps him on a dive state.

Grace is God's reconciliation with the world through Christ's crucifixion as is rightly captured, "For if when we were enemies (corrupt) we were reconciled to God through the death of His Son, much more having been reconciled, we shall besaved by His life (Romans. 5:10). Grace is a spirit that helps us to take pleasure in infirmities, in reproach, in needs, in persecutions, in distress for God's sake. It is a spirit of strength and to resist un-godliness.

"And I will pour on the house of David and the inhabitants of Jerusalem the Spirit of Grace and

Supplication; then they will mourn for Him as one mourns for his only son, and grieve for Him as one grieves for a firstborn" (Zechariah. 12:10).

A man of grace is someone that is favorably inclined. It is all by grace. As it was also written, For the Lord God is a Sun and a Shield; the Lord will give grace and glory; no good thing will He withhold from those who walk uprightly. Grace is a spirit of empowerment. Grace is a divine backing.

Grace is the power of God's ministry in a man. "Not that we are sufficient of ourselves to think of anything as being from ourselves but our sufficiency is from God, who also made us sufficient as ministers of the new covenant (spirit), not of the letter (law) but the Spirit; for the letter kills, but the spirit gives life (2 Corinthians. 3:5-6). It is the grace of God that lifts us when we are down.

Grace means favor, graciousness, kindness, beauty, pleasantness, charm, attractiveness, loveliness, affectionate regard and mercy of God. No man can be this and still live a corrupt life.

God's grace upon someone's life enables him to look longingly to God in all things. God's grace results in seeing Him as God of infinite mercy.

Grace is the Spirit of God that makes man live holy. It draws us near Christ, convicts us of sin, and causes us to do the will of God, assures us of salvation and helps to live a victorious life. Through understanding and the prayer of grace according to God's will, we share Christ with others in the same grace and truth. Grace is God's part of a person that enables him to behave like Him. There can be no darkness in Light (grace).

The effective operating power of God's grace becomes ineffective in the life of anyone who trusts in his efforts. It is all by grace. It is all according to the election of grace; it was said to Paul (Eph. 1:5, 11; Matt. 11:25, 26; Jn. 15: 16, 19).

In Him, we have redemption through His blood, the forgiveness of sins, according to the riches of His grace (Ephesians. 1:7). This (grace) is a surpassing divine backing. "For by grace have been saved through faith, and that not of yourselves, it is the gift of God, not of works, lest anyone should boast" (Ephesians. 2:8-9).

But to each one of us, grace was given according to the measure of Christ's gift (Ephesians. 4:7). This includes you. Being with Jesus in sincerity is a work of grace. "Grace abides with those who love the Lord Jesus Christ in sincerity (Ephesians. 2:6).We can say no to corruption.

Grace is the sufficient mercy of God with which strength is made perfect in weakness. Grace is not in effect at our salvation but God's manifestation power, and love that make salvation possible.

When someone's character is under question, the grace of God becomes his or her enablement. "And he said to me (Paul), 'My grace is sufficient for you' for my strength is made perfect in weakness" (2 Corinthians. 12:9).

I will strengthen the house of Judah, and I will save the House of Joseph, I will bring them back because I have mercy on them (Zechariah. 9:6). That is grace! There is nothing grace cannot do. It is God's grace that brings salvation. "For the grace of God that brings salvation has appeared to all men, teaching us that denying ungodliness and worldly lusts, we should live soberly, righteously and godly in this present age (Titus. 2: 11-12).

We must fully acknowledge that by the working grace of God is anyone able to come fearfully out of sin/corruption.

Grace is not God's permission to sin and sin again that God is merciful to forgive. Without a reverse of such order of act is ungodliness. Grace is growing in godliness.

When we backslide, it should not be a continuous something. We have already entered into a relationship with God that abounds. Let us quickly realize our mistakes and come back to God at once without repetition of the same mistakes; that is grace and what it does.

Grace gives salvation; the prospect of salvation is great. The glories of grace is inexpressible, as it was written, "...of this salvation the prophets had inquired and searched carefuly who prophesied of the grace that would come to you, searching what or what manner of time, the spirit of Christ who was in them was indicating when He testified beforehand the suffering of Christ *and the glories that would follow* (1 Peter. 1:10-11).

A call to salvation is by His grace a calling to holiness and blessings. His grace is sufficient to escape corruption

(f)

AVOID TEMPTATION AND OBJECTS OF TEMPTATIONS

To befall temptation is to be enticed into something evil. It is when it is a desire to sin. It is a force that attracts a person into sinful lifestyle and to become a victim of that sin and the reward. Temptation can come to a person in different forms as a test or trial. However, in whichever way it may come, there is always a way to escape.

We are not tempted in an area not so precious or essential, and everyone is tested at his time. The precious a destiny is, the tougher the temptation so that we may not resist it.

Adam and Jesus Christ (the new Adam) faced the same temptations of three-manifold bits of intelligence. Jesus resisted all, but Adam yielded and brought upon human race sin and death. Jesus resisted the devil resulting in justification and eternity.

The devil is deceptive; he knows the three human weaknesses:

(a)   The Problem of the flesh and stomach

(b)   The problem of the eyes concerning everything that is pleasant to the eye and thirdly:

(c)   Pride; that is, man's desires to equal himself with others and God in powers and wisdom, leading to disobedience and corruption

The above three manifold bits of intelligence of this world, in summary, is <u>lust</u>:

1. "The tree was good for food" (Genesis. 3:6); the devil also commanded Jesus Christ: 'command these stones to become bread' (Luke. 4:1-13) – this is a stomach problem.

2. The lust of the eye – "The tree was pleasant to the eyes"; also the devil showed the new Adam all the wealth of the kingdoms – things pleasant to the eyes.

3. The last temptation was pride. The devil knew that man likes to equal himself to others and to God. "A tree desirable to make one wise" was presented to Adam while the same devil said to Jesus: "throw yourself down from here if you are the son of God (Matthew. 4:6) -

pride, but Jesus answered and said to him, "it is written 'you shall not tempt the Lord your God.'"

Jesus swallowed pride even though he is the son of God. Men are corrupt and perish because of the lust of the flesh, eye, and pride.

Both Adam and Jesus faced three same temptations, Adam yielded, bringing upon human race death but the new Adam resisted justifying us.

The temptation is a snare. Understand the rationale in every sin/temptation. The purpose of every temptation is to make us sin so that we will be disqualified from the glory of God and be qualified for hell.

When you are faced with temptation, look unto God hopefully that He can deliver you. Temptation enslaves someone when he failed that he should not be able to free from its mastery and has had a victory over him. All unrighteousness is a sin, and there is no sin not leading to death (1 John. 5:17).

The Lord is not slack concerning His promise, as some count slackness, but is long surffering towards us, not willing that any should perish but that all should come to repentance (2 Peter. 3:9).

To be able to avoid temptation, we engage the mystery of grace.This is the mystery of deliberate resistance to an object of temptation. "Let us, therefore, come boldly to the throne of grace that we may obtain mercy and find grace to help in time of need (Hebrews. 5:16).

Have it in mind that every temptation is a double edge sword that destroys man-kind and our glory. In the instance of Jesus, "he... Jesus was led up by the Spirit into the wilderness to be tempted by the devil. To be tempted from the perfect point means a positive test. From the devil's point, it implies enticement to sin, from Jesus' point of view it is a challenge from Satan to test God's sovereignty and plan. Whenever we are tempted, we look unto Jesus about temptation.

In order not to be tempted, look unto Jesus, upon whom the ends of the ages have come (1 Cor. 10:11), that he will not allow you to be tempted beyond what you can bear, as with the temptation will also make the way of escape that you may be able to escape from it.

Deliberately refused to be tempted, Daniel refused to be defiled (Daniel. 1:7). Study the word of God to prove you before that temptation comes (2 Timothy. 2:3). Avoid the lust of this world (Romans. 13:14) which are objects of temptations, resist the devil, using the hammer and the rock to break his head and the temptation (James.4:7). Then exercise your will power through the grace of God He lavished on us to avoid sin and objects of temptation (Matthew. 5:27-29; Proverbs. 14:15).

You have the power to say no to the evil inside you. When you failed to condition yourself the devil will come forth and mess you up without resistance. Have a no-go area for yourself. Our lifting power is in our overcoming power. Say no to corruption.

(g)

AVOID COVETOUSNESS

Covetousness means lust. It is the wanting of something by hurting others and at the expense of others with the motive of jealousy or envy whether it concerns an ox, a pen, a sheep, money, food or clothing or for any lust or self-interest.

Stealing is covetousness. "Let him who steals steal no longer; but rather let him labor, performing with his own hands what is right, in order that he may have something to share with him who need (Ephesians. 4:28). Covetousness causes corruption.

Why greediness? Is it not because of the constant unhealthy desire for sexual things? *Growth and progress is stages in life patiently wait:*

When a baby is born, he or she has to grow into adulthood. The biological parents have to know and prepare for the child needs till adulthood.

Growth is a providential journey of going higher and higher in what we have from God. Financial growth is like when we were born as a child, then we grew, and matured to death.

This godly development starts at the stage of conception to when we say to each other, good bye.

(h).

OBSERVING THE LAW AGAINST THE VIOLENCE: KILLING AND KIDNAPPING

The law concerning violence is well stated in the book of old and new Testaments. Thou shall not kill, and thou shall not kidnap. We are admonished not to strike a man to death (Exodus. 21:12)

He who kidnaps a man and sells him if found in his hand shall surely be put to death (Exodus. 21:16); remember to observe the law and all shall be well with you. We *keep away this evil among us. (Deuteronomy. 24:7). Live a corruption free life.*

(i)

ACKNOWLEDGE THE SIN AND STAY OFF QUICKLY

Do not hide evil.This helps to fight corruption. Acknowledge your inclination to sin. Bring it out into the light and dealt with it. Make restitution and turn your trust wholly in God who can keep you from falling (Jude. 1:24) and it is His desire to forgive.

God in His mercy (Acts .7:11) commands us to deal with sin straightforwardly and thoroughly. Only through acknowledging sin and seeking forgiveness we can be set free from sin (the corruption of this world).

Holiness is the power of condemnation to sin. The Lord has separated us to Himself to walk in His way. He calls us, therefore, to be holy as He is holy, but yet iniquity brings that separation. He called us on His voice and said "…you shall be Holy to me, for I the Lord am holy, and have separated you from the people that you should be mine" (Leviticus. 20:26) meaning, stay off sin quickly

(j).

WALKING IN THE SPIRIT OF LOVE

This is the greatest law. Love is when all you want is to see others happy, even if you are not part of their progress. Love is not when you are only in a giving position. Many can give without loving, but God mind for us is always to love (1 John. 4:8).

The opposite of love is hatred. Thou shall not hate thy brother in your heart (Leviticus. 19:17). God is good. He repays those who hate Him to their face, to destroy them. He will not be slack with him who hates Him; he will repay him to his face. Therefore you shall keep the commandment, the statute, and judgments which he commands you today, observe them (Deuteronomy. 7:7-11).

Just imagine that scriptural reference, He is God of mercy, but He repays those who hate Him to their face. How do we show that we hate God? The things of God and that of the devil are two different thing.

Any act which is outside the will of God is a show of hatred for Him. We show that we hate God through disobedience. God is not just loving He Loves (1 John. 4:7, 8). Love is not a description of God; it is the essence of God. We try every day to know what God says about love.

Not that we have loved God that He loves us. His quality of love can be understood as the unselfish giving of oneself for the highest good of another. His love is not capricious, sentimental and mere romanticism, but a steadfast choice to be others centered.

Love is the golden ruling scepter of God. His love is multifacet. He said, "my presence will go with you, and I will give you rest" (Exodus. 23:14). That is the essence of His love. Tell me the person that has ever shown the above portrayed passionate affection for you; such is the divine love we find when we know God. When we walk in the spirit of love we should able to live corruption free life. Love is when all we want is to see others happy and fulfilled even though we are not part of it.

(k)

FORBID THE DOG AND THE HARLOT

The dog and the harlot are not permitted to practice their evil on the land God has given to us. Fight this evil in your land. Do away with this corruption from your home as a Hebrew and seed of Abraham, Isaac, and Jacob, the generations that have served God.

"There shall be no ritual harlot of the daughters of Israel, or a perverted one of the sons of Israel" (Deuteronomy. 24:17).

You shall not bring the wages of a harlot or the price of a dog to the house of the LORD your God for any vowed offering, for both of these are an abomination to the LORD your God (Deuteronomy. 23:18). Resist the sin of dogging and harlotry.

Women and men of God are not permitted to become prostitutes. A female prostitute is identified <u>as a harlot,</u> and a male prostitute is identified <u>as a dog.</u> Christianity and legislation prohibited prostitution and money obtained by that sinful means to be given as a vowed offering to the LORD.

Thou shall not bring sin to the house of God and on the land God has given to you to live, "For all who do such things, all who behave unrighteously are an abomination to the LORD your God" (Deuteronomy. 25:16). We are advised to stop this corruption in our land.

(l) Resist Stealing Spirit:

It is not in the character of God's children to steal. "When you come into your neighbor's vine yard, you may eat your feel of grapes at your pleasure, but you shall not put any in your container" (Deuteronomy. 23:24).

Stealing is not in the character of a good person. This is one of the reasons good people are entrusted with power, and they dominate at anywhere they are because they are truly good people. Sir, you are. Stop stealing public funds.

CHAPTER EIGHTEEN

EXCLAMATION OF THE BOOK

In which area I have sinned against you, LORD, I am truly sorry. Forgive me so that I would have the courage, and the faith to serve you forever.

I admitted that we were sinners, that we have went wrong and had done things we know we should not do. Turn us away from sin and restore us.

Watch not those shadows which our flesh gathered outside your will even when you called us to godliness, to purity so that we do not stumble and goes stray from you and perish.

Recognize not our limitations (sinful life) as we step out boldly with obedience from those limitations that are barriers to our relationship with you.

God we pray thee, never fail to save and provide all that are needed to establish us who come to you for forgiveness and for your work.

We courageously turn from ungodly patterns of life with the faith you will protect and provide for us from your provisions that comes in an unconventional way from an unexpected source-meaning you are a miracle God.

Man fails when he chooses the lust of the eye, the lust of the flesh and the pride of this world that is deceptive. Those things tempt us today, but God calls us apart that we might work ever with Him as our God. We must be quick to ask God's forgiveness and repentance as we admit we do things we know we should not do even though the devastation that accompanies sin is great. May God give us the grace to do his will.

PART 3

THE VALUES WE CREATE

&

SHARE

CHAPTER NINETEEN

ZERO BASE SUCCESS

Man is a light that needs three component things to shine and retain its fullness. This component thing is a right attitude; self-control and the fear of God.These things add value to life in fullness and overcome darkness.

Man's relationship with people is in correlation with his relationship with God. Whether it is power or knowledge, is of no value when it cannot fix and save others.

Life is about donation. Success is not in the accumulation of wealth measures in the hands and bank account without lifting others with it; but a fulfilment arose in impacting others to actualize in life.

Success and greatness is not necessarily the much that is bequeated to children except when what is bequeathed is properly harnessed; then it makes great!

Inheritance without a dream is a waste.

Many people are looting, doing evil to be rich and famous all for a reason their children should not suffer the way they did and live below poverty level. No! This is not a legacy. Who said the children would not suffer the consequences of this evil deed, or subsequently be poorer and hunger-stricken? Do we know excess wind fall can make us learn only consumption behavior which leads to poverty?

When children see their parents as spend thrifts, they learn from them. Looted money is not valued and it's spent carelessly. It is the worst ever spent. Stolen waters quench thirst, but it is the worst ever drank, food eaten in secret is delicious; but it causes stomach disorder. This is the behavior of stolen money.

Nobody has ever stolen and still claim to be trusted, great and better than others without condemnation.

 But who is greater (Luke. 22:25- 27) as it is written..., "he who sits at the table or he who serves? Is it not he who sits at the table? I am among you as the one who serves".

Here, Jesus redefined the meaning of greatness and reversed the values, principles, standards, ethics, and idea of the world about greatness to be measured in the line of good service, not even a thought of idleness and unearned riches.

The background of one's parents does not count in pursuing success; it is by predestination everyone is born into a particular family. One cannot choose a biological father while as we have the freedom to choose a spiritual pathway that will make us great!

Our future sees beyond where we are coming from. We ought to start at a very humble beginning to a greater height and allow God to take the front seat of our drives.

We do not allow the one penny of today to snatch our big future. Looted wealth is the worst ever spent by man. Let our children learn, let them work, and be free from violence and tell them free things are most times, not precious things.

Anything that has value has price to be paid to get it. Teach children the proper use of money, so they do not grow up becoming spend thrifts.

Tell them to relate well with their families and others.

*Let them learn how to work and earn money from jobs/ self-developments serve God with it and give to those in nee*d. Teach them not to allow money to become the lord of their lives. We must rescue our generation from this nonsense.

Let me point out some personalities of some of our forefathers: Isaac, Abraham, Jacob, Elisha etc).

Isaac did not only lived on his father's (Abraham) wealth but he also planted and harvested a hundred fold in a single year on the land he inherited from his father.

Jacob did not depend on the wealth of his father Isaac, but he lived on the covenant platform of the blessing for him.

He sent his children to Egypt with money to buy grain during that economic meltdown, at the period when the power of money failed in Israel.

Jacob's water well in Samaria has today become a reference in the Bible (John. 4:6) at where Jesus met the Samaritan woman for water.

Elisha was from a wealthy home, his father had twelve yokes of oxen engaged in plowing, yet he did not allow his son to grow up grasping. It was while Elisha was usefully engaged in the performance of his duty, *undertaking the strenuous work of plowing that he received a divine call.* Elisha was a farmer who lived with his parents (1 king. 19:16-21). He maintained his own house in Samaria (2kings. 6:32)

David was sent for in the bush to lead is people; these are few riddles with meaning so teach your children the proper way to live a life.

We all know that poverty (deficiency in resources) is not good. In the first place, there is nothing wrong with men possessing wealth. A good man leave inheritance to his children's children; but the wrong comes in when wealth possesses their owners.

Wealth of sinners is laid up for the just (Proverbs. 13:12).

Proverbs 10:15 also demonstrated that the rich man wealth is his strong city (strength). It is a good thing to be wealthy, but the wrong comes when riches ruin men.

Train a child in the way he should go, and when he is old, he will not depart from it

(Proverbs. 22: 6). We do not profane our children's destinies by making them mere spend thrifts. Tell them money earned is better than giftr and to love. The venom of a viper does not harm a tortoise. Work does not kill.

Make good use of your time and weaknesses and stop doing the wrong things. We need money because it gives us a voice. Let's put our hands and knowledge at work together to earn us some money. Teach our children love, how to work and a peaceful way to follow one another.

Are our children prepared to inherit us ? It is the well trained children that will take the inheritance as in the instance of the following story?

The only son of a certain wealthy man was to inherit the father's wealth/businesses when he shall die. The elder gave him one condition to be met: Go and earn ten thousand dollars and bring it to me. My multi-million dollars business will be handed to your when I shall die. "You shall manage my businesses", the old man added.

In no long time, his son brought him the money he had collected from his mother, claiming he worked for it. Though his father welcomed him and collected the money from him, and threw it inside his burning oven. The two watched the oven until the money was burnt to ashes.

The old man told his son to go and work for fifteen Thousand dollars and bring it to him. After many weeks, he came back to the father with the money. His mother had given him the money again and told the boy to wait for some times without eating food so he could look disguised in the sight of his father. He did as he was instructed by his mother.

When he met his father with the money, he took the cash (fifteen thousand dollars) from him and threw it into the burner, and they watched the fifteen Thousand dollars burnt to ashes.

Then he told his son to go and work to earn Five Thousand Dollars this time and bring it to him again.

The boy went and met his mother for advice. Many options were decided out to raise this money by the mother to outsmart the old man; but at last, the boy decided to go and earn the Five Thousand dollars and give it to his father. He refused her mother's advice at this time.

The boy now traveled to another town where he did hard plowing and menial jobs to get the money. He went very far to places nobody knew him as a child of a wealthy man.

He at this time worked for the money. He spent months denied himself unnecessary spending and pleasures of the flesh and stopped all sort of luxury life accustomed to some children born and raised in a rich Family just to save the Five thousand dollars.

When he finally came home, his mother could not recognize her son. She burst into tears and murmured "What a wicked Father!" but the boy was excited about working and saving Five Thousand dollars by himself to give to his Father.

With that desperate condition, he quickly went and presented the money to his father who was again incidentally using the burner/oven.

He gave his father the money, and again he threw it inside the burning oven; but the boy shouted, "Daddy!" and dived to the oven and brought the cashout and exclaimed: Daddy! Don't burn it! The father asked him, why should I not burn this one?

The son answered and said: we do not waste money. We do not allow our sweat to be lavished and carelessly. The father then said: you have worked for this money my son. Nobody will stand looking, watching his effort being burnt, wasted as we had done in the previous ones. It was your mother that gave you the money before.

Friends! Inheritance without a dream is a waste.

Train yourself and your family on the proper way to use money so that they do not grow up to be looters and only spend thrifts.   Many Looters and spend thrifts hardly know how to manage money in the Economy. They print more money when it got finished.

The truth is that the economic power of one's parents can influence his/ her child's ascendancy and put him or her on a right direction to go in life.

When such economic power and intellect are well utilized on a child, his or her future, as well as the society will be safe.

Why do we engage in corruption that kills? Someone does not have to steal /kill to be great. We need God and people to live, do your best to stop indulging in corruption and indecent lifestyle.

What is refer to a zero base success is the rising from nothing to something in grace and truth without covetousness. I believe we will choose to have this success.

We do not allow our background to put our back to the ground or poison our future with the pain of the past due to poor background that ruptures dreams and success.

God never consults our past to determine our future. A man may be needy now, poor or sick in the body and yet a friend of God marked for success. We have a cause to live. A person who has a cause to champion bears and understands that venom does tortoise no harm, we work into greatness with understanding and working hard.

Success is always hard to attain and makes someone feel like quitting. If we want to reach the peak, we must cherish small beginning, humble ourselves, and we will experience Fulfilment.

We do not become great to start; we start very small and become very great. When a Person thinks too big to start with a little he may be too big and heavy for a lifting by God. Small opportunities are often the beginning of greater enterprise.

Success is fulfilment in accomplishment after the sacrifices made to overcome oppositions we encountered, the struggles against overwhelming odds and the courage with which we have maintained focus.

Someone can achieve success effortlessly even while in the valley. A person in a valley looks up for lifting not down.

Difficulties are builders. There has never been somebody who has never have a define moment so love challenges because this encourages us to do more.

A person without a problem is a dead man. A challenge is a twig to higher height. The sky should be our starting point, not even our limit.

'A challenge is resistant that says to us; we would n't get there when we are going.' a resistance we displaced for lasting breakthrough. Those resistances may include: fear, ignorance, We cannot, I can't, self-deception, people will say, and what people would say, poverty, I have not known much;

but know that you will never have all you need to start, start working to show the little you have known. You can start it now.

Success is like a case won. A case won is a problem put to rest and every problem solved becomes a case study/ reference. Our success can be a reference from which others learn.

folded hands fail and have no glory for not fulfilling a course. Wake up! I am not speaking against wealth but when craving for idle hands wealth which result into corruption.

"Money is a defense" (Ecclesiastes.7:12). The love of it makes one go wrong. We do not have to earn a bad name and demean our selves because of money.

We do not have to travel afar before we become the kind of person we chose to be. The fortunes we are looking outside for is in us. We have over one billion mineral deposits inside us untapped. With this believe, we can defeat others drive.

Avoid "I must travel out of my country" mentality. This desperate desire has destroyed many destiny. Some people once traveled and missed their opportunities while some could not go back home.

Perhaps, I do not see traveling to far places for fortune as the only solution or an end to a struggle or lack. Some people often think that their destiny is in a specific place.

All Adam needed in the Garden of Eden to be happy was inside him unknown. *Eve was inside Adam unknown to him until she was formed out of him.* All we need to achieve in life are inside us , at where we are, and we do.

I can see the gold you are looking for inside you (a very titanic idea is in you unknown, it is creativity). Are you following me? ***Tire Ni O!*** (All is yours o!).

This believe (I must relocate without seeking God's opinion) can destroy a great destiny. Our destiny is inside us, It is located anywhere we are. There is nothing in a far country if we are not led by God comparable with what God has for us at where we may be. We can make where we are today sightseeing. We should emancipate ourselves from slavery. None but our God and minds can free us

Russia President, Vladimir Putin as he has rightly said, "Africa is a cemetery for Africans. When an African becomes rich, his bank accounts are in Switzerland. He travels to France for medical treatment.

He invests in Germany. He buys from Dubai. He consumes Chinese. He prays in Rome, or Mecca. His children study in Europe. He travels to Canada, USA, and Europe for tourism.

If he dies, he will be buried in his native country of Africa. Africa is just a cemetery for Africans. How could a cemetery be developed?"

Hold on to what is around you and the opportunities you have. Where we are is not the problem but what we do with it in this century of global connections for rapid development.

Do you know opportunity may lie within the smallest undiscovered opportunity around you? Do what you can with what you have at where you are and you will have a good success. May God open our eyes.

The way we think may also be one of the reasons we may find no end, meaning that we are our minds which makes and bring us what we want.

Our destiny is control by two forces, *you and God.* If we succeed, it is God and we; but when we have failed, we are held responsible because God does not fail.

Are you currently the unsuccessful among the successful? Is it so? Good! Listen to this: behind every successful man there is a lot of unsuccessful years. A successful man was an unachieved person. That you may not have succeeded does not mean you are failure. One day is one day. Just keep trying.

Pray to God .When we pray God comes in.

Friends!

If we see a person or a nation that is greater than we are, we fine out what is it they do we do not do. May God give us better understanding.

Success is also in knowing something nobody else knows which we know, then we do it.

Let every man has an appointment with himself and with God. Winners always see the strength of God in battles.

Some people also believe that they can only be lifted by bringing someone else down. Stop pulling people to failure. That is witchcraft hurting. Stop fighting others. That is not the ground rule to fulfilment.

Do you know a person that loves and kind is joyful and fulfiled because he is doing the Lord's will? He may not be fulfiled even when he is given a house or a car or a place of prominence.

Don't go wrong because of position or money (the third principal actor of this world). Remember that vanity of vanities, says the preacher; all is vanity (Ecclesiastes. 12: 8).

Start from a zero base and know that sudden success and working outside God's will is none sense. We can say no to corruption when we realize that with God's grace we can do all things and be more than conquerors.

What house are we going to build in exchange for the soul that is so precious? If our pleasures are not in godliness, forget it.

Comment: In the above chapter the entire mood of the author is aligned. The preacher has not found and seen anything of lasting value in man's life outside salvation. Then why should a man choose evil because of worldly things since life itself is vanity?

What house can someone build just for pleasure in exchange for the soul? If our treasures are not in line with God's plan for us, forget it: info.jeafservices@gmail.com

'Perhaps, I do not think to travel to far places is the solution or an end to a struggle or lack.

Some people often think that their destiny is in a specific place. It is everywhere. It might be closer than you ever think.

All Adam needed to be happy were inside him unknown.

Eve was inside Adam's body unknown to him until she was formed out of him.

What you need to achieve in life and

to be fulfiled in your endeavor are inside you.

Extract it! And Stop going everywhere'

CHAPTER TWENTY

ADDRESSING THE PROBLEM OF OVER DEPENDENCE/ RELIANCE

The above topic under discussion (over dependence) is one of the reasons public funds are stolen by some people to meet dependants needs. Africa as an instance is a country where people rise up telling the whole world over two million people are dependent on them for a living. What is glorious about carrying liabilities?

Not to teach others self reliance is an added problem to us. Teach them how to fish. We should agree that by giving people money, we only make the problem bigger, harder to solve and more deadly. It is like when someone is giving a hungry person that is sick a medicine without meal to sustain him because food is essential to also keep him.

We may end up killing that person. I use the above assertion to emphasize the importance of being on guard and to know the difference between those who give to give others freedom and those who give to kill others through giving. An educated nation full of beggers is the name used to describe a country full of people not working. Do not hang your life on others. This is not in the original culture of man. There is joy in labor.

Indolence: Workers provides and supply in the summer. Indolence is a folly; folding hands brings poverty and poverty causes disobedience, corruption and violence. It brings temptations and jealousy.

Working hands never slumber. There is dignity in labor. Learn how to do some handwork, and thy LORD will bless that work of your hands.

No matter how severe shall the famine; those who do not rely on others survive it because they consider the ways of the ants (Proverbs 6:6). Indolence (lassitude) deprives someone of livelihood. The youth are encouraged here to work hard and smart to the right direction.

The good thing is that we still have small time to prepare to avoid being victim of the next coming global Economic meltdown due to global economic changes coming up as a result of technology. It is not a long time from now. Only the corruption free nations shall survive it. Many people will go for it mostly the unprepared nations. It is only those who are prepared that will survive it.

Many do not teach people how to fish, but they sell people to sharks that swallow them up. We want people to learn how to fish.

Look inward, be creative, be scientific and develop methods. Let us shift our minds from share the money attitude which is corruption to, let us make people with our money. Let us shift our minds from steal the money.

In my conclusion, this looting culture needs a standard law to be stopped. Lack of sound financial handling policy has contributed to the extreme financial corruption in Africa and in other many parts of the world.

I and, 'Addressing the Societal Problem: corruption and creating values in Africa' is concerned because most people/ countries do not choose to learn to manage their own money, they do not learn to invest their own money and develop and grow through skills acquisition. Most of them squander their money and beg others to give them their own money. Moreover, Instead of learning, they simply turn their money over to indecency and wrong financial advisers that cheat on them and begin to beg for bread later.

Majority of people drink too much and lack average financial literacy quota needed by an average person to excel in business. This bad habit takes their earning and steals their future. Millions of them may be in the bar drinking now with their take-home pay and stolen public funds. We need a very sound financial usage policy in Africa, mostly in Nigeria.

When God put the government of His people on my shoulders, I will not abuse it; we can do this together.

CHAPTER TWENTY ONE

ABORTION IS WRONG:

From the moment of conception, life is formed and there is a progressive development of this cell that continues to adulthood.

To terminate this foetus without a reasonable excuse (e.g. in a typical critical situation when one life can save another for the two not to die) is unrighteousness and every unrighteousness is sin. Life begins at conception. Abortion is definitely wrong. It is an indefinite termination of life. The Bible says that life begins at conception (God fashions us while in the womb).

Psalm 139:13 says: for you confirmed my inward parts, you cover me in my mother's womb. What does not confirm God's law is not conformed.

Unnecessary abortion is a bad practice. To be frank, the Bible is not more specific on the issue of abortion because such a practice was unthinkable to the people of God. All through the Old Testament, women yearned for children a s gift from God and no one prayed to be barren. Then no righteous woman or lady or a person destroy his child? It was an act of paganism to the peak.

Idea of killing a child (abortion) is an anathema to a reasonable person. The same is still occurring today, it is an ongoing phenomenon in many hospitals, and some people have even learned how to do abortion as a profession. This is a terrible blot and acting this way, we admitted that human beings are not worth anything.

From the moment of conception, on there is a progression of development that continues through adulthood. Abortion is wrong

(Disciple. Eraga E.Jacob)

CHAPTER TWENTY-TWO

WHICH HOUSE WILL YOU BUILD IN EXCHANGE FOR THOU SOUL?

God does not dwell in clay and temples made with hands. Heaven is His throne, and the earth is His footstool. What house will you build for God in exchange for your soul? Some people may be committing evil to make money (shadows).

We make people with money we do not make money with people. Then why should we do things that will put people into indulgence and destruction? Don't we understand?

What house will you build for Him, what vehicle you will buy for Him? Has God not all those things and gives the power to make wealth?

But Solomon built Him a house, however the highest does not dwell in temples made by men or with hands (Act.7:49); (Isaiah. 66:1, 2)

Is it because of money and power we should accept doing the wrong things you ought not to do? Because of money and popularity, someone is killing others, telling lies and kept not the commandments and the laws of God.

You kill those who tell the truth, you starve them, kidnap them and you sent on fire to the sacrament and holy place. You gnash at those that preach salvation. They cry out to God yet you run after them with your swords. You share blood. However, the highest God will never live in your house, the fleet of cars and jets you have are all clay and I will never accept it from you. I will rather trek to the temple and preach the word of grace and truth.We the family of God will not ask you for anything.

Look around and think about the natural disasters that are coming to those shadows (the pride of this world). Vanity! True joy is found in God. True prosperity is in salvation, and true financial prosperity is in helping others to actualize.

Divine wealth does not cause tensions and evil. It does not make unnecessary noise and destructions. It does not host evil and it does not bribe and sponsor wickedness.

If "Nebuchadnezzar" gave us food, we would not eat it. We will reject it. If you Pharaoh shall give us food to eat, Israel will go to the mountain to seek God's face and renew his strength.

Because of money, a supposed child of God has chosen to walk out from Him. The army of God is now found in the drinking parlor, evil sect, etc. Wealth is now defying a titan of peace. Who are you?

We need God to have wealth; but we do not need wealth to have God. "If surely you serve me, I will be with you." "If you willingly follow me, you shall be blessed and blessing I will bless you said the Lord of the host.

Remember that there is no comfort zone in this world except the zone where God is resident. The earth is your footstool (door), and heaven is your home. Say no to evil,

What house will you build on earth when you sow evil? Say no to the shadows of this world and corruption.

Set apart for God, reserved for God and His service since nothing that is polluted could be worthy of ventilation. Purity becomes a big part of God's Holy call for you.

I promise you, if you walk in the light of God and willing to keep walking right, eventually, you will not only enjoy financial prosperity but true fulfilment.

'Say no to corruption'.

The benefits in stopping corruption practice are:

- God takes over your country and your home

- Stealing, killing and suffering is destroyed

- Blessings are preserved

- You rise from good for nothing to something great

- You enter your divine inheritance

- You feel in power and retain it

- You enjoy protections effortlessly

- You flourish , and your nation will be exalted

- You becomes the undividable , and the unbeatable

- You earn respect

- The whole world will hear you, listing to you, and respect you and the Lord you serve.

- Crises are minimized greatly.

- Peace, love and unity are guaranteed.

CHAPTER TWENTY-THREE

DISCIPLINARY ACTION IS A WEAPON FOR LIVING RIGHT

Discipline entails giving instruction, to scourge and to be rebuked which means to undertake physical training measures upon some one who is disobedient to a constituted authority.

All discipline begins with verbal instruction to be obeyed. This may be what a child/ a person needs to have a proper training and positive change.

It is placed upon parents and government by God to discipline their children / a person responsibly. This discipline is to inculcate the fear of God or the authority in the person or a child. When a person is obedient, he or she has been prepared to be peaceful and prosper. The worst rebellious people on earth are disobedient people.

Parents/authorities should be careful in their disciplinary tools. There are times when verbal instruction is what is only needed to correct a person, not sparking words and torturing as this may lead to willful rebellion.

Parenting/ leadership is a difficult and a double edge sword task responsibility. It comes in a child upbringing and to an adult. Parents and leaders are advised to discipline their children/ citizens' recalcitrant and to appropriate accurate disciplinary measures on them.

It is not also wrong to caution and corrects a corrupt person using the word of God because the word of God reprimands and does not despise and discouraged discipline. As it is written:

"My son, do not despise the chastening of

the LORD, nor be discouraged when you are

rebuked by Him; for whom the LORD loves

He chastens, and scourges every son whom

He receives" (Hebrews 12:5-6)

Discipline: Discipline is a good weapon for fighting corruption. Without discipline, we can do nothing. With only some discipline we can solve only some problems. With total discipline, we can solve all problems totally.

Do not underestimate the importance of discipline because discipline is a too that make things to work by force when diplomacy failed.

Open your children to discipline. A disciplined child is a child loved. Discipline enables a child to go the right way and learn how to resist evil, oppression and abounds.

Learning to abound requires never forgetting that God is the one who has made the difference (Philippians. 4:12, 19). This kind of positive training is remembering and is final testing and necessary because without discipline our flesh will be tempted, pride will follow, and with this, our intended good purpose on earthwill be ruined. Be disciplined.

CHAPTER TWENTY FOUR

THE PERPLEX:

- When nails grow long, you cut the nails not the fingers.

- When misunderstanding grows up, cut the ego not your relationship.

- Don't worry about things you cannot control.

- There are six simple rules to be happy: See God in all things, free your heart from hatred, free your mind from worries, live simple, give more but expect less.

- I do not need someone who only sees the good in me; I also need someone who sees the bad   side of me and still wants me so that I can change.

- Nothing is perfect, that is the reason a pencil has an eraser

- Believe in yourself even when everyone else does not.

- People with good intentions make promises, but it takes those with good attitude to make them a reality.

- Stop wishing, start doing.

- Pretense is the worst inner enemy of a man, be real.

- One small positive talk in going to bed can change a life

- He who knees before God can stand before anyone. I knee before you Lord.

- A snail can sleep for three years without getting starve. Work, you are not a snail.

- If you are not losing friends, then you are not growing new friends.

- Class mate is per time. Time defines who your class mate is.

- Mentally talking to yourself during a task is reasoning and a good way to keep focus. Be focus.

- Be thankful for the bad things you escaped in life, for they opened your eyes to the good things you were not paying attention to.

- After so many years of your education, yet you complained of no job. There is nothing like a job in the Bible, I see work; so find your work.

- Pastor Enouch Adeboye left his *job* for his *work* when he found no job in the Bible.

- Opportunities come after a huge sacrifice. Decide it.

- Do what you want to do; it is not always what others want you to do.

- Love is not when there are no fights in a relationship. Love is when once the fight ends, love is still there and there.

- There are three rules or principle for realization:

(1). Know your work.

(2). Give your best but do not reveal ever thing you know at once.

(3)..?

- There is a currency very valuable for making money; it is 'time.'

- The strongest people are not those who show strength in front of us, but those that win battles for us unknown, and we know

- You do not need a reason before you help someone.

- Beauty is not about having a pretty make face. It is about having a pretty mind, heart, character and brain

- Your problem is not the problem. Your response is the problem.

- Be such a dope soul that people crave your vibes.

- Actualization is the best revenge.

- The mirror is my best friend because it does not cry when I laugh. It Laughs!

- Losing is a learning experience. It teaches you patience, meekness and how to work harder. It is a powerful motivator.

- The most dangerous creature on earth is a fake relation.

- Geniuses always look crazy to the average mind- Millionaire mindset.

- Whatever we want most in life, first give it out. It will come to us back in hundredfold.

- Success is not how much money you have, it is to be attracted by the kind of person we are.

- Sometimes we have to move on without certain people. If they are meant to be part of our lives they will catch up.

- Never work with a person who is desperate for money without understanding else you both get crashed.

- It is better to be hated for what we are than to be loved for what we are not. There are fake people everywhere on earth. You are who?

- Respect yourself enough to walk away from anything that no longer serves you, grow you, or makes you happy.

- Your best value is when you meant something to someone. Quit where you add no value.

- No one deserves to be an option, but some chose to be.

- Distance does not ruin a relationship, but lies and doubt does.

- God has perfect timing for everyone: never early, never late and takes a little patience and faith.

OTHER BOOKS WRITTEN BY DISCIPLE ERAGA E JACOB

- The Bowl of Treasures" (*An insight to light)*

 - The Wonders of Grace

- Titanic Ideas (Think outside the Job & Your Employer's Box)

- Fame to Fulfilment (The Secrets to Achieving Fulfilment)

THE AUTHOR:

A Person You Should Know: Disciple Eraga E. Jacob

- Don't look back when you should not. Don't stress over things that don't matters. Don't worry about things you cannot manage.

- God will wreck your plans when He sees that your plans will wreck you

Disciple Eraga Jacob is a man of grace; plain, and has an insight to the revealed truth.He strongly believes in God, and that all puzzles of life answer to God in a mystery.

He swaps the world with his <u>stringent anti-Corruption crusade Movement</u> through the preaching of the message (Word) of Grace and truth (John .1: 17), walking against ungodliness for salvation (unspotted life).

In undertaking this phase of the divine order, the Disciple uses different medium which includes hand bills, audio CD, tapes, books, elocutions for his out-reach changing the world.

Disciple Eraga Jacob hobbies are: Reading, Running, Reasoning and Writing (RRRW).He has written several books on different endeavors impacting lives. He hates excuses, what only sees the reasons we cannot proceed, and sees discouragement as the courage to work harder. He is also a synonym of kindness, and he rules his **word.**

Eraga Jacob is a minister, a teacher and a resourceful entrepreneur. His registered trade mark is AIJ.

Mrs. Eraga Faith Lawrenta is his wife. Their marriage is blessed with children: Abraham, Isaac & Jacob Jnr. They love almost as much as he does

Ino.jeafservices@gmail.com,jacobabrahamisaa

c@yahoo.com